# Easy Grammar Grade 4

# Student Test Booklet

*Wanda C. Phillips*

**Easy Grammar Systems**

SCOTTSDALE, ARIZONA 85255

Printed in the United States

© 2006

# TABLE OF CONTENTS

**TESTS**

**A.  Sentence Types:**
   **Directions:**  Write the sentence type on the line.

1.  _____    Go slowly.

2.  _____    Is that your cat?

3.  _____    My balloon popped!

4.  _____    She makes dolls.


**B.  Capitalization:**
   **Directions:**  Write a capital letter above any word that should be capitalized.

1.  did governor ruiz read <u>indian in the cupboard</u> to your class at aztec school?

2.  the visitor from spain spoke to the rotary club about the mexican war.

3.  has mom bought berryland* iced tea and african daisies at caremart company

   on cole avenue in taneytown?

4.  one student asked,  "is the erie canal in new york?"

5.  dear pam,

      my dad and i will attend prescott pioneers day in june.

                              your friend,

                              paco


**C.  Common and Proper Nouns:**
   **Directions:**  Place a ✓ if the noun is common.

1.  ____    TURTLE        3.  ____    BEAGLE      5.  ____    SUPERMAN

2.  ____    ATLANTA       4.  ____    CANADA      6.  ____    BRICKLAYER

1

**D.  Concrete and Abstract Nouns:**
    **Directions:**  Place a ⊠ if the noun is abstract.

1. ___  fear        2. ___  faith     3. ___  fig     4. ___  forest

**E.  Singular and Plural Nouns:**
    **Directions:**  Write the correct spelling of each plural noun.

1. berry - _____        5. replay - _____

2. tax - _____        6. sofa - _____

3. mouse - _____        7. gas - _____

4. deer - _____        8. patch - _____

**F.  Possessive Nouns:**
    **Directions:**  Write the possessive.

1. room belonging to his sister - _____

2. an office used by more than one woman - _____

3. wading pool shared by two toddlers - _____

**G.  Identifying Nouns:**
    **Directions:**  Circle any nouns.

1. Three movies about birds of the desert were shown at our library yesterday.

**H.  Punctuation:**
    **Directions:**  Insert needed punctuation.

1. No we wont be moving to Purdy Washington

2. Kama asked  Was Emma born on Thursday May 20 1982

3. They hope to sell forty two tickets for our teams carnival by 4 30 today

4. By the way wash your ears face and neck with this suds free soap

5. His new address is 22 Brook Avenue Nyles MI   49102

### I. Subjects and Verbs:
**Directions:** Underline the subject once and the verb or verb phrase twice.
**Note:** Crossing out prepositional phrases will help you.

1. A package from Emily arrived before dinner on Friday.

2. A nurse and an aide helped the patient into bed.

3. Four of the girls looked at the stars during the outdoor party.

4. Come inside the house through the front door.


### J. Contractions:
**Directions:** Write the contraction.

1. were not - _____   3. I have - _____   5. would not - _____

2. they will - _____   4. will not - _____   6. what is - _____


### K. You're/Your, It's/Its, and They're/Their/There:
**Directions:** Circle the correct word.

1. Take ( there, their, they're ) picture.

2. I think that ( you're, your ) upset.

3. Let me know when ( it's, its ) time to leave.


### L. Subject-Verb Agreement:
**Directions:** Underline the subject once. Underline the verb that agrees twice.

1. Your idea ( sound, sounds ) interesting.

2. The woman with the huge green glasses ( take, takes ) orders.

3. His brother and she ( hikes, hike ) everywhere.


### M. Irregular Verbs:
**Directions:** Underline the subject once and the correct verb phrase twice.

1. The dog was ( lying, laying ) on the porch.                    3

2. Parker had ( rode, ridden ) her horse fast.

3. She has ( ate, eaten ) lunch.

4. I could have ( run, ran ) more than fifty yards.

5. We were ( given, gave ) large red markers.

6. My pencil is ( broke, broken ).

7. Have you ( did, done ) your homework?

8. We should have ( set, sat ) our lunches in the ice chest.

9. The bell may have already ( rang, rung ).

10. Kama's balloon had ( busted, burst ).

**N. Tenses:**
   **Directions:** Underline the subject once and the verb or verb phrase twice. Write the tense in the blank.

1. _____ The child colored a picture.

2. _____ You will turn left at the next street.

3. _____ Their dad is a beekeeper.

**O. Usage and Knowledge:**

1. Circle any infinitive that is a regular verb:   to flash   to fly   to flip

2. Circle the interjection:   **Wow!  This soup is hot and spicy.**

3. Circle the possessive pronoun:   **The girls are enjoying their new puppy.**

4. Write the antecedent of the possessive pronoun in sentence 3:   _____

5. Circle the conjunction:   **Yikes!  Mo or Bo has fallen in the stream.**

6. Circle the correct answer:   We haven't received ( no, any ) money.

7. Circle the correct answer:   My brother acts ( strange, strangely ) sometimes.

4

8.  Circle the correct answer:   I didn't play very ( good, well ) in the first game.

9.  Circle the correct answer:   Are you feeling ( good, well )?

**P.  Identifying Adjectives:**
   **Directions:**  Circle any adjective.

1.  One elderly lady wore silver sandals with many stones and a low heel.

**Q.  Degrees of Adjectives:**
   **Directions:**  Circle the correct answer.

1.  The fifth storm was ( more violent, most violent ).

2.  This is the ( uglier, ugliest ) mask of the two.

3.  You are ( more creative, most creative ) than I.

**R.  Adverbs:**
   **Directions:**  Circle any adverbs.

1.  My friend talks too loudly sometimes.

2.  They never go anywhere early.

**S.  Degrees of Adverbs:**
   **Directions:**  Circle the correct answer.

1.  Paco runs ( faster, fastest ) in his high school.

2.  Kit answers the phone ( more politely , mostly politely ) than his brother.

3.  When we travel, Aunt Jo stops ( more often, most often ) than Uncle Bo.

**T.  Pronouns:**
   **Directions:**  Circle the correct answer.

1.  ( Me and Lana, Lana and I, Lana and me ) made a clay pot.

2.  Don't hit Jacob and ( I, me )!

3. The scouts must take ( his, their ) canteens.

4. ( They, Them ) attend a rodeo every year.

5. Our grandparents and ( we, us ) are going to Idaho.

6. The baker fried the doughnuts ( hisself, himself ).

7. Matt left with Sarah and ( she, her ).


**U. Nouns Used as Subjects, Direct Objects, and Objects of the Preposition:**
   **Directions:** Look at the boldfaced word. Write **S.** for subject, **D.O.** for direct object, and **O.P.** for object of the preposition.

1. ____ During the **winter**, Tara skis.

2. ____ Give the **rattle** to the baby.

3. ____ After the parade, our **family** went to a café for lunch.

Name_____    **Verb Test**

Date_____

A.  Directions:  Write the contraction.

1.  they are - _____    4.  I am - _____    7.  you are - _____

2.  cannot - _____    5.  he is - _____    8.  I shall - _____

3.  they have - _____    6.  did not - _____    9.  will not - _____

B.  Directions:  Write <u>Yes</u> if the boldfaced verb shows action; write <u>No</u> if the
                    boldfaced verb does not show action.

1.  _____  The priest **kneels** at the altar.
2.  _____  She **became** a firefighter.
3.  _____  His mother **whistles** often.
4.  _____  Roy and Frances **skydive**.
5.  _____  Mr. Collins **is** nice.

C.  Directions:  Write <u>RV</u> if the verb is a regular verb; write <u>IV</u> if the verb is irregular.

1.  _____ to say    3.  _____ to shop    5.  _____ to see
2.  _____ to live    4.  _____ to stand    6.  _____ to hope

D.  Directions:  Circle the correct verb.
1.  The track star had ( run, ran ) a great race.
2.  Brett has ( did, done ) his guitar lesson.
3.  Have you ( saw, seen ) a hummingbird?
4.  Pioneers had ( rode, ridden ) across the desert in covered wagons.
5.  Has your brother ever ( drunk, drank ) flavored iced tea?
6.  Several branches must have ( fallen, fell ) during the storm.
7.  You should not have ( swam, swum ) by yourself.
8.  The accident victims were ( flown, flew ) to a nearby hospital.
9.  Our cat has ( laid, lain ) on the sofa all afternoon.
10.  He has ( sat, set ) the video on the front seat of his car.
11.  The lawyer ( lay, laid ) her pen by a note pad.

12. Have you ( ate, eaten ) yet?

13. Their friend has ( came, come ) by train.

14. Please ( raise, rise ) the flag.

15. We ( brang, brought ) our sleeping bags.


E. Directions:   Write the tense of the boldfaced verb or verb phrase.

1. _____   He **studies** every day.

2. _____   John and Eric **studied** for an hour.

3. _____   I **shall study** this map.

4. _____   Carla **washed** her car with hot, soapy water.

5. _____   Diana **sponges** spots from her carpeting.


F. Directions:   Circle the correct word.

1.  Are you aware that ( it's, its ) time to leave?

2. Does ( you're, your ) play open tonight?

3. ( They're, Their, There ) very happy.

4. Several girls refused to give ( they're, their, there ) apples away.

5. The cat licked ( it's, its ) sore paw.


G. Directions:   Circle the verb that agrees with the subject.

1. Many cast iron kettles ( hang, hangs ) in front of the antique shop.

2. A rhinoceros ( has, have ) one or two horns on his snout.

3. That chef ( stir, stirs ) fried green onion into the stew.

4. One of the boys usually ( hit, hits ) the ball to left field.

5. Those ladies ( is, are ) on a bus tour.


H. Directions:   Cross out any prepositional phrases.  Underline the subject once and
the verb/verb phrase twice.

1. A woman waded in the lake.

2. The family will eat at a cafe.

3. The road leads to an old barn.

4. She washed her hair and dried it.

5. Before the meeting, they must have talked about their decision.

10

## A. **Preposition List:**
Directions:   List forty prepositions.

1. _____

2. _____

3. _____

4. _____

5. _____

6. _____

7. _____

8. _____

9. _____

10. _____

11. _____

12. _____

13. _____

14. _____

15. _____

16. _____

17. _____

18. _____

19. _____

20. _____

21. _____

22. _____

23. _____

24. _____

25. _____

26. _____

27. _____

28. _____

29. _____

30. _____

31. _____

32. _____

33. _____

34. _____

35. _____

36. _____

37. _____

38. _____

39. _____

40. _____

## B.  **Object of the Preposition:**
Directions:   Cross out any prepositional phrases.  Label the object of the preposition - O.P.

1.   Your coat is on the floor.

2.   Janell looks for baseball cards.

C. **Compound Subjects:**
   Directions:   Cross out any prepositional phrases.  Underline the subject once
                 and the verb/verb phrase twice.

1.   His bat and ball are in the garage.

2.   Phoenix and Sacramento are capital cities.
🍓🍓🍓🍓🍓🍓🍓🍓🍓🍓🍓🍓🍓🍓🍓🍓🍓🍓🍓🍓🍓🍓🍓🍓🍓🍓🍓🍓🍓🍓🍓🍓🍓🍓🍓🍓🍓🍓🍓🍓🍓🍓
D.   **Imperative Sentences:**
     Directions:   Cross out any prepositional phrases.  Underline the subject once
                   and the verb/verb phrase twice.

1.   Go to the store, please.

2.   After lunch, mail this envelope
🍓🍓🍓🍓🍓🍓🍓🍓🍓🍓🍓🍓🍓🍓🍓🍓🍓🍓🍓🍓🍓🍓🍓🍓🍓🍓🍓🍓🍓🍓🍓🍓🍓🍓🍓🍓🍓🍓🍓🍓🍓🍓
E.   **Compound Objects of the Preposition:**
     Directions:   Cross out any prepositional phrases.  Underline the subject once
                   and the verb/verb phrase twice.

1.   He left without a jacket or sweater.

2.   Flowers are growing by the shed and barn.
🍓🍓🍓🍓🍓🍓🍓🍓🍓🍓🍓🍓🍓🍓🍓🍓🍓🍓🍓🍓🍓🍓🍓🍓🍓🍓🍓🍓🍓🍓🍓🍓🍓🍓🍓🍓🍓🍓🍓🍓🍓🍓
F.   **Compound Verbs:**
     Directions:   Cross out any prepositional phrases.  Underline the subject once
                   and the verb/verb phrase twice.

1.   I moved furniture and cleaned.

2.   Matt writes stories and sends them to his grandpa.
🍓🍓🍓🍓🍓🍓🍓🍓🍓🍓🍓🍓🍓🍓🍓🍓🍓🍓🍓🍓🍓🍓🍓🍓🍓🍓🍓🍓🍓🍓🍓🍓🍓🍓🍓🍓🍓🍓🍓🍓🍓🍓
G.   **Infinitives:**
     Directions:   Cross out any prepositional phrases.  Underline the subject once
                   and the verb twice.  Place an infinitive in parenthesis (  ).

1.   I like to talk.

2.   Wolves need to wander.
🍓🍓🍓🍓🍓🍓🍓🍓🍓🍓🍓🍓🍓🍓🍓🍓🍓🍓🍓🍓🍓🍓🍓🍓🍓🍓🍓🍓🍓🍓🍓🍓🍓🍓🍓🍓🍓🍓🍓🍓🍓🍓
H.   **Direct Objects:**
     Directions:   Cross out any prepositional phrases.  Underline the subject once
                   and the verb/verb phrase twice.  Label any direct object-D.O.

1.   Jake milks cows in the morning.

2.   The college student purchased towels for his new apartment.

12

Name_____     **Noun Test**

Date_____

## A. Concrete and Abstract Nouns:

Directions:   Write C if the noun is concrete;  write A if the noun is abstract.

1. _____ love          3. _____ applesauce      5. _____ faith

2. _____ air           4. _____ kindness        6. _____ boat

## B. Common and Proper Nouns:

Directions:   Write CN if the noun is common; write PN if the noun is proper.

1. _____ HUDSON BAY    4. _____ COLORADO        7. _____ JUNK

2. _____ FIREPLACE     5. _____ VERDE RIVER     8. _____ MARY

3. _____ CANADA        6. _____ FRUIT BAR       9. _____ LAKE

## C. Noun Identification:

Directions:   Underline any nouns in each sentence.

**Remember:**   You may wish to circle determiners to help you find most nouns.

1. Josh's dad is a fireman in Washington.

2. Has your brother gone with his friends?

3. An elephant was used in that movie.

4. Whose coats are lying on these two chairs?

5. Some lively children are swinging in those magnolia trees.

6. In June, our family will take many short trips to the beach.

7. No fruit was served at Judy's breakfast on Saturday.

### D. Singular and Plural Nouns:

Directions: Write the plural.

1. bulb - _____

2. penny - _____

3. tooth - _____

4. wish - _____

5. calf - _____

6. mouse - _____

7. carp - _____

8. bay - _____

9. bus - _____

10. roof - _____

11. tomato - _____

12. fez - _____

### E. Possessive Nouns

Directions: Write the possessive form.

1. a package that belongs to Andy

_____

2. a path for horses

_____

3. a club belonging to more than one woman

_____

4. skates belonging to Frances

_____

5. a playground belonging to more than one child

_____

4

A. **Prepositional Phrases:**

Directions:   Cross out any prepositional phrases.  Underline the subject once and the verb/verb phrase twice.  Label any direct object - <u>D.O.</u>

1. Jack eats lunch at a cafe.

2. The fence behind the barn is broken.

3. Kirk lives in West Virginia.

4. Chimes resounded through the church.

5. Paula left without her lunch bag.

6. In the middle of the afternoon, his grandmother always naps.

7. Hide this under the bed until the party.

8. Has the weaver woven another rug?

9. Everyone except the hostess gathered around the table.

10. The temperature in Phoenix rises above one hundred degrees during the summer.

B. **Compounds:**

Directions:   Cross out any prepositional phrases.  Underline the subject once and the verb/verb phrase twice.

1. A telegram arrived for Annette and Mario.

2. He signed a card and placed it inside an envelope.

3. The bank's manager and a teller met with the couple.

4. Mrs. Sands loves to cook and often invites friends for dinner.

5. Either Jane or her sister attends a technical school.

6. A teacher read an article about drugs and alcohol to his class.          15

7. His father and mother own a small house outside the city limits.

8. She ordered fries and a hamburger without pickles or onions.

C. **Contractions:**

Directions: Write the contraction.

1. I shall - _____    6. they have - _____

2. does not - _____   7. is not - _____

3. you will - _____   8. what is - _____

4. she is - _____     9. could not - _____

5. must not - _____   10. I am- _____

D. **Action?:**

Directions: Write <u>Yes</u> if the boldfaced verb shows action; write <u>No</u> if the boldfaced verb does not show action.

1. _____ Cream-filled doughnuts **are** delicious.

2. _____ Jeff **threw** a baseball.

3. _____ The pastry chef **tasted** his dessert.

E. **Regular or Irregular:**

Directions: Write <u>RV</u> if the verb is regular. Write <u>IV</u> if the verb is irregular.

1. _____ to choose   3. _____ to growl   5. _____ to make

2. _____ to frown    4. _____ to ring    6. _____ to chew

F. **Subject-Verb Agreement:**

Directions: Circle the verb that agrees with the subject.

1. Several airplanes ( dusts, dust ) crops in that area.

2. One of their friends ( works, work ) in an ice cream shop.

3. Megan and her mother ( shops, shop ) often.

4. The man in line with his three children ( paint, paints ) houses for a living.

G. **Tenses:**

Directions:   Write the tense (present, past, or future) on the line provided.

Note:   You may want to cross out prepositional phrases, underline subject once, and verb/verb phrase twice to help determine the tense.

1. _____ Joel and she are good friends.

2. _____ A queen will attend that celebration.

3. _____ Mozart was a famous composer.

4. _____ Joanna planned her own wedding.

5. _____ His father explores caves on weekends.

H. **Irregular Verbs:**

Directions:   Circle the correct verb.

1. His brothers have ( drank, drunk ) all of the soda.

2. Where has the team ( went, gone )?

3. A ring had been ( stole, stolen ) from the jewelry store.

4. Many party favors had been ( bought, boughten ) for the party.

5. Andy was ( chosen, chose ) to video the event.

6. The newspaper is ( laying, lying ) in the driveway.

7. A small tree has ( grew, grown ) by the road.

8. The patient ( lay, laid ) on his back during surgery.

9. Has she ( shook, shaken ) the rug in her room?

10. He may have ( came, come ) to the airport in his own car.

Date_____

A.  **Adjective Identification:**

    Directions:  Circle any adjective.

Suggestion:  First, look for limiting adjectives.  Then, reread the sentence searching for descriptive adjectives.

1.  Small, rusty nails lay on the broken bench.

2.  These jelly doughnuts are good.

3.  During our zoo trip, we saw many monkeys.

4.  The red brick house was built in ten months.

5.  Their little turtle now lives near a marshy pond.

6.  An orange tissue box is on that counter.

7.  The bride wore a white silk gown with short, puffed sleeves.


B.  **Degrees of Adjectives:**

    Directions:  Circle the correct answer.

1.  Kimberly is the ( taller, tallest ) person in her Sunday school class.

2.  Let's sit in that area; it is ( grassier, grassiest ) than this one.

3.  This rubber band is ( more elastic, most elastic ) of the six that you gave me.

4.  During the fourth performance of the play, we did ( goodest, best ).

5.  This car attendant is ( more agreeable, most agreeable ) than his partner.

6.  A steel plow was ( lighter, lightest ) than the old iron type.

7.  She is the ( nimbler, nimblest ) gymnast in her group.

8.  The garlic odor is ( pungenter, more pungent ) than the onion smell.

A. **Prepositional Phrases:**

> Directions: Cross out any prepositional phrases. Underline the subject once and the verb/verb phrase twice. Label any direct object - <u>D.O.</u>

1. A surfer dashed across the sand.

2. Put these old coins into a drawer.

3. Two bicyclists pedaled along a path.

4. Jarred placed a house key under a rock by the front door.


B. **Compounds:**

> Directions: Cross out any prepositional phrases. Underline the subject once and the verb/verb phrase twice.

1. A card for Mom and Dad arrived in the mail.

2. The toddler took his first step and fell.

3. A cashier and customer talked about the new science museum.

4. Rob sneezed lightly and coughed.


C. **Contractions:**

> Directions: Write the contraction.

1. are not - _____     5. where is - _____

2. I am- _____     6. had not - _____

3. might not - _____     7. they have - _____

4. we are - _____     8. I would - _____


D. **Action?:**

> Directions: Write <u>Yes</u> if the boldfaced verb shows action; write <u>No</u> if the boldfaced verb does not show action.

1. _____ We **shivered** from the cold.

2. _____ She **remained** calm during the earthquake.          21

E. **Regular or Irregular:**

Directions: Write <u>RV</u> if the verb is regular. Write <u>IV</u> if the verb is irregular.

1. _____ to write     2. _____ to wash     3. _____ to fly     4. _____ to work

F. **Subject-Verb Agreement:**

Directions: Circle the verb that agrees with the subject.

1. That puppy ( whimper, whimpers ) so much.

2. Opals ( is, are ) very soft stones.

3. One of the boys ( skate, skates ) often.

G. **Tenses:**

Directions: Write the tense ( present, past, or future ) on the line provided.

Note: You may want to cross out prepositional phrases, underline subject once, and underline the verb/verb phrase twice to help determine the tense.

1. _____ He lost his wedding ring.

2. _____ A pianist will play for us.

3. _____ I am happy.

4. _____ The merchant gives coupons to his customers.

H. **Irregular Verbs:**

Directions: Circle the correct verb.

1. He has ( began, begun ) a new job.

2. You should have ( took, taken ) a different route.

3. She has ( swum, swam ) on the team for three years.

4. The actress must have ( flown, flew ) on an earlier flight.

5. That fork has been ( lying, laying ) in the sink for two days.

6.  The patient had ( brung, brought ) X-rays with her.

7.  Have you ever ( went, gone ) to Canada?

8.  The curtain has been ( tore, torn ) from the rod.

9.  We could not have ( ran, run ) further.

10. They must have ( drank, drunk ) our juice.


I. **Abstract and Concrete Nouns:**
   Directions:  Write <u>A</u> if the noun is abstract; write <u>C</u> if the noun is concrete.

1. ____ hammer   2. ____ feelings   3. ____ shampoo   4. ____ love


J. **Common and Proper Nouns:**
   Directions:  Write <u>CN</u> if the noun is common; write <u>PN</u> if the noun is proper.

1. ____ city   2. ____ wheel   3. ____ street   4. ____ Lund Avenue


K. **Noun Plurals:**
   Directions:  Write the plural form.

1. delay - _____      6. zero - _____

2. prize - _____      7. catch - _____

3. deer - _____       8. dress - _____

4. fireman - _____    9. dairy - _____

5. scarf - _____      10. mother-in-law _____


L. **Noun Possessives:**
   Directions:  Write the possessive form.

1. a bottle belonging to a baby - _____

2. toys shared by several babies - _____

3. a playground shared by more than one child - _____

23

M. **Noun or Adjective?:**
   Directions: If the boldfaced word serves as a noun, write <u>N</u> in the space. If the boldfaced word serves as an adjective, write <u>A</u> in the space.

1. _____ Please return this book to the **library**.

2. _____ What did I do with my **library** card?

3. _____ A **balloon** cluster was sent as a birthday gift.

4. _____ A **balloon** was tied to their mailbox.

N. **Noun Identification:**

   Directions: Circle any nouns

Suggestion: You may want to underline determiners to help you locate nouns.

1. A pole was decorated with eight red hearts and several streamers for the party.

2. His small car was parked next to your uncle's recreational vehicle.

3. For that party, Mom set our table with fine china and fancy glasses.

O. **Sentence Types:**

   Directions: Write the sentence type ( declarative, interrogative, imperative, or exclamatory ) in the space.

1. _____ A baker from Vienna made the first bagel.

2. _____ Will they shop for new shoes?

3. _____ Stack those boxes here, please.

4. _____ Finally!  We've received the bonus!

P. **Conjunctions and Interjections:**

   Directions: Write Conj. above any conjunction; write Intj. above any interjection.

1. Yeah!  Marcy and Tom are coming with us!!

2. Alice or Yvonne may decide, but they must make their decision quickly.

24

Name_____     **ADVERBS**
                                              **Test**

Date_____

A.  Circle any adverbs that tell **how**:

1.  He answered calmly.

2.  They play well together.

3.  A baby smiled sweetly at us.

B.  Circle any adverbs that tell **when**:

1.  Must you leave soon?

2.  The children eat popcorn nightly.

3.  Yesterday, Anne and I arrived late for work.

C.  Circle any adverbs that tell **where**

1.  Have you seen Sue's magazine anywhere?

2.  Here is Aunt Faye's high school yearbook.

3.  You may come in, but leave your boots outside.

D.  Circle any adverbs that tell **to what extent**:

1.  This food is too salty and very dry.

2.  We're so happy about your news.

3.  You are not quite as stubborn as your brother.

E.  Circle the correct adverb form:

1.  When the four girls competed, Shana won ( more easily, most easily ).

2.  She finished ( earlier, earliest ) of all the contestants in the race.

3.  This gray kitten laps milk ( more steadily, most steadily ) than the white one.

4.  The older girl stood ( more quietly, most quietly ) than her little sister.

5.  I worked the math problem ( more carefully, most carefully ) the second time.

## A.  **Prepositional Phrases:**

Directions:   Cross out any prepositional phrases.  Underline the subject once
and the verb/verb phrase twice.  Label any direct object - <u>D.O.</u>

1.  The child hid under the table.
2.  Brad pushed a pen between the cushions of the sofa.

## B.  **Compounds:**

Directions:   Cross out any prepositional phrases.  Underline the subject once
and the verb/verb phrase twice.

1.  A robin and swallow flew across the lawn.

2.  We tied the gift with ribbon and a silk flower.

3.  A shopper looked at jewelry and bought a necklace.

## C.  **Contractions:**

Directions:   Write the contraction.

1.  I shall - _____

2.  could not- _____

3.  you are - _____

4.  here is - _____

5.  what is - _____

6.  is not - _____

7.  they are - _____

8.  did not - _____

9.  are not - _____

10.  I have - _____

## D.  **Common and Proper Noun:**

Directions:  Find a proper noun for the boldfaced common noun.
Write the letter of the proper noun in the space.

1.  _____  *S TATE*      (A)  COUNTY     (B)  TEXAS          (C)  REGION

2.  _____  *PERSON*   (A)  BANKER     (B)  GOLFER        (C)  LAURA

E. **Subject-Verb Agreement:**

Directions:   Circle the verb that agrees with the subject.

1. They often ( has, have ) hot chocolate for breakfast.

2. His ferrets ( eats, eat ) cereal.

3. Dad seldom ( buy, buys ) new shoes.

4. One of the women ( bring, brings ) an umbrella every day.


F. **Tenses:**

Directions:   Write the tense ( present, past, or future ) on the line provided.

**Note:**  You may want to cross out prepositional phrases, underline the subject once, and underline the verb/verb phrase twice to help determine the tense.

1. _____   A bull stood inside a fence.

2. _____   Many want to blow bubbles.

3. _____   They will drive to Idaho.

4. _____   I shall stay here.

G. **Irregular Verbs:**

Directions:   Circle the correct verb.

1. The child had ( grew, grown ) four inches.

2. Have you ( brung, brought ) your lunch?

3. The show must have ( began, begun ).

4. These rugs have not been ( shook, shaken ).

5. Sandals were ( worn, wore ) on the hot sand.

6. She should have ( ran, run ) faster.

7. Hot dogs were ( took, taken ) on the picnic.

28

8. Shannon might have ( rode, ridden ) her horse to the park.

9. Their team should not have ( beat, beaten ) us.

10. Many ice cubes were ( froze, frozen ) in plastic trays.

## H. **Noun Plurals:**

Directions:   Write the plural form.

1.  bunch - _____          6.  toy - _____

2.  cactus - _____          7.  woman - _____

3.  roof - _____          8.  potato - _____

4.  life - _____          9.  bush  - _____

5.  gate - _____          10.  story - _____

## I.  **Noun Possessives:**

Directions:   Write the possessive form.

1.  a football belonging to a boy - _____

2.  a football shared by three boys - _____

3.  a jersey belonging to a player - _____

## J.  **Noun or Adjective?:**

Directions:   If the boldfaced word serves as a noun, write <u>N</u> in the space.  If the boldfaced word serves as an adjective, write <u>A</u> in the space.

1.  _____        Our **door** knob is jammed.

2.  _____        Please open the **door**.

3.  _____        Your **television** is large.

4.  _____        That **television** screen seems small.

K. **Noun Identification:**
Directions: Circle any nouns.

Suggestion: You may want to underline determiners to help you locate nouns.

1. Your shoes with green laces are in the closet.

2. He ate two pancakes, an egg, and a muffin for breakfast.

L. **Sentence types:**
Directions: Write the sentence type ( declarative, interrogative, imperative, or exclamatory ) in the space.

1. _____ No!  Our dinner is burned!

2. _____ Please tell me the truth.

3. _____ The tile is cracked.

4. _____ May I read this book?

M. **Adjective Identification:**
Directions: Circle any adjectives.

1. A tall, thin model smiled at the audience.

2. Few ice storms occur in this area.

3. Her long black hair is pretty.

N. **Degrees of Adjectives:**
Directions: Circle the correct adjective form.

1. Of all the bird eggs, this is ( tinier, tiniest ).

2. The cake is ( more delicious, most delicious ) than the pie.

3. She is ( short, shortest ) in her family.

4. Division was my ( more difficult, most difficult ) part of math.

5. He is the ( taller, tallest ) one on his team.

30

Name_____    **PRONOUNS**
                                        **Test**
Date_____

Directions:   Circle the correct pronoun.

1.  My friend and ( me, I ) like to roller skate.

2.  The shirt purchased for ( he, him ) was too small.

3.  Are Joy and ( I, me ) allowed to come, too?

4.  The leader and ( they, them ) attended a meeting.

5.  Yesterday, Scott and ( us, we ) read three short stories.

6.  From ( whom, who ) did you receive birthday cards?

7.  Ashley saw ( they, them ) at the beach.

8.  Several waitresses counted ( her, their ) tips.

9.  Each of the ladies drove ( her, their ) own car.

10.  The report about frogs was written by ( she, her ).

11.  ( Who, Whom ) won that race?

12.  Please stand between Jim and ( I, me ).

13.  Help ( us, we ) to do this job, please.

14.  The pebble hit ( he, him ) on the leg.

15.  Herb, Janice, and ( she, her ) entered the contest.

## A. **Prepositional Phrases:**

Directions: Cross out any prepositional phrases. Underline the subject once and the verb/verb phrase twice. Label any direct object - <u>D.O.</u>

1. His mom and dad like salads with cheese.

2. One boy slid down the slide and fell on the sand.

3. Do you want to go with Gregg and me?

4. Sit by the fire for a few minutes.

## B. **Contractions:**
Directions: Write the contraction.

1. will not - _____     6. does not - _____

2. cannot- _____       7. they will - _____

3. where is - _____     8. I would - _____

4. were not - _____     9. should not - _____

5. I am - _____         10. we are - _____

## C. **Common and Proper Nouns:**
Directions: Write <u>CN</u> if the word is a common noun; write <u>PN</u> if the word is a proper noun.

1. _____ MUSIC          3. _____ NAIL

2. _____ FLORIDA        4. _____ MEXICO

## D. **Concrete and Abstract Nouns:**
Directions: Write <u>A</u> if the noun is abstract; write <u>C</u> if the noun is concrete.

1. _____ hair           3. _____ friendship

2. _____ sadness        4. _____ napkin

E. **Subject-Verb Agreement:**
    Directions: Circle the verb that agrees with the subject.

1. Many children ( plays, play ) at the beach.

2. Each person ( has, have ) to bring his own lunch.

3. One of the golfers ( hit, hits ) the ball very hard.

4. Penny and Katie ( shop, shops ) together.


F. **Tenses:**
    Directions: Write the tense ( present, past, or future ) on the line provided.

1. _____ This car needs new tires.

2. _____ Her hat blew into the street.

3. _____ Nancy will bring her new dog along.

4. _____ Jackie and Craig live near us.


G. **Verb Phrases:**
    Directions: Underline the entire verb phrase.

1. David must have realized his mistake.

2. May I help you?

3. Janet had been given five dollars.

4. The pastor should not have talked so long.


H. **Irregular Verbs:**
    Directions: Circle the correct verb.

1. Joy has ( came, come ) to see you.

2. A truck driver had ( took, taken ) the package.

3. Jeremy must have ( ate, eaten ) the last piece of pie.

4. Your book is ( lying, laying ) on the table.

34

5. Their neighbor has ( went, gone ) to England.

6. He had not ( spoke, spoken ) for several minutes.

7. The children had ( swam, swum ) all afternoon.

8. Susan's baby has ( drank, drunk ) his entire bottle of milk.

9. They must have ( rode, ridden ) their bikes to school.

10. The sun has ( rose, risen ).

11. Their team has ( flown, flew ) to Michigan.

12. The judge was ( sworn, swore ) into office.

13. ( Set, Sit ) the groceries here on the counter.

14. Have you (did, done ) your homework?

15. Chad must have ( took, taken ) his roller skates with him.

I. **Noun Plurals:**

Directions: Write the plural form.

1. gulf - _____     6. man - _____

2. radish - _____     7. window - _____

3. lane - _____     8. tomato - _____

4. worry - _____     9. bus - _____

5. tooth - _____     10. monkey - _____

J. **Noun Possessives:**

Directions: Write the possessive form.

1. a wallet belonging to Kathy - _____

2. birthday cards given to a girl - _____

3. a basketball shared by two boys - _____

K. **Noun Identification:**

   Directions:   Circle any nouns.

   Suggestion:   *You may want to underline determiners to help you locate nouns.*

1.   The lovely bride danced several slow dances with her smiling father.

2.   Two brown rabbits sat beneath a rose bush in Tony's front yard.


L. **Sentence types:**

   Directions:   Write the sentence type ( declarative, interrogative, imperative, or exclamatory ) in the space.

1.   _____   Let's eat!

2.   _____   Is dinner ready?

3.   _____   Dinner is ready.

4.   _____   Wash your hands before dinner.


M. **Adjective Identification:**

   Directions:   Circle any adjectives.

   **Remember:**   Find both limiting and descriptive adjectives.

1.   That young man met three friends for a birthday lunch.

2.   Many large palm trees grow by their old house near the ocean.


N. **Degrees of Adjectives:**

   Directions:   Circle the correct adjective form.

1.   Jane's sister is ( taller, tallest ) than she.

2.   The peach ice cream was ( more delicious, most delicious ) than the vanilla.

3.   Of the five houses on our block, ours is ( smaller, smallest ).

4.   Mr. Jackson's fifth son is ( more athletic, most athletic ).


O. **Adverb Usage:**

   Directions:   Circle the correct word

1.   Her friend runs ( slowly, slow ).

2. He didn't get ( none, any ).

3. That man is acting ( strange, strangely ).

4. They don't want ( anything, nothing ).


P. **Degrees of Adverbs:**

Directions:   Circle the correct adverb.

1. Henry runs ( faster, fastest ) than Jerry.

2. My grandmother sews ( more neatly, most neatly ) than her sister.

3. She works ( harder, hardest ) of all the employees.

4. The printer did his third job ( more quickly, most quickly ).


Q  **Pronoun Usage:**

Directions:   Circle the correct pronoun.

1. Chris and ( me, I ) need to sweep.

2. Does ( he, him ) need an answer today?

3. ( We, Us ) would like to speak with you.

4. Can you help ( they, them )?

5. Put your books beside Terry and ( I, me ).

6. The scout leader and ( them, they ) went camping.

7. A dog followed ( we, us ) around the playground.

8. Carey went with Lance and ( her, she ) on vacation.


R.  **Conjunctions and Interjections:**

Directions:   Label any conjunction - CONJ.; label any interjection - INTJ.

1. A doe and a fawn walked in the open meadow.

2. Hurrah!  Our team tied for first!

3. You may take a small bag or backpack, but pack two heavy sweaters.

Date_____

Directions:   Write the capital letter above any word that needs to be capitalized.

1.   the bear paw mountains are forty miles from canada.

2.   did the westinghouse company start the first radio station?

3.   our family celebrates christmas at grandpa barton's house.

4.   their teacher read <u>doll in the garden</u>.

5.   the man asked, "do you like kringle's corn flakes?"

6.   he attends a baptist church by marsh creek.

7.   dear miss rankin,

      have a great trip to mission beach on friday.

                              truly yours,
                              tom hulse

8.   i.  types of art

         a.  pop art

         b.  cowboy art

9.   will micah attend hillsdale college in michigan?

10.   our family had a picnic on independence day in july.

11.   a poem by j. ciardi begins, "the morning that the world began."

12.   in history, i learned about an organization called the green mountain boys.

13.   did mother learn french during the summer she learned to play the piano?

Date_____

Directions:   Insert needed punctuation.

| | |
|---|---|
| **period (.)** | **exclamation point (!)** |
| **apostrophe (')** | **hyphen (-)** |
| **comma (,)** | **underlining ( _ )** |
| **colon (:)** | **quotation marks (" ")** |
| **question mark (?)** | |

1.  Yes she does live in Tustin California

2.  Juan said   Come in

3.  Yeah   Our dog won first prize

4.  This dungeon by the way was once used

5.  They sold their home on Friday Sept  6  1996

6.  Sally may we take your little sisters skates with us

7.  Big Cowboy Western is her favorite book

8.  Jims uncle works at a childrens playground

9.  We need the following for our games     two balls a jump rope and prizes

10.  Dear Hattie
       We will arrive at 2 00 P M
          Sincerely
          Victor

11.  They live at 4663 E Grove Street  Richmond VA   23226

12.  The lady said   I picked twenty two buckets of cherries today

**A.  Sentence Types:**
  **Directions:**  Write the sentence type on the line.

1. _____    Go slowly.

2. _____    Is that your cat?

3. _____    My balloon popped!

4. _____    She makes dolls.


**B.  Capitalization:**
  **Directions:**  Write a capital letter above any word that should be capitalized.

1.  did governor ruiz read <u>indian in the cupboard</u> to your class at aztec school?

2.  the visitor from spain spoke to the rotary club about the mexican war.

3.  has mom bought berryland* iced tea and african daisies at caremart company

    on cole avenue in taneytown?

4.  one student asked,  "is the erie canal in new york?"

5.  dear pam,

      my dad and i will attend prescott pioneers day in june.

                      your friend,

                      paco


**C.  Common and Proper Nouns:**
  **Directions:**  Place a  ✓  if the noun is common.

1. ____   TURTLE      3. ____   BEAGLE      5. ____   SUPERMAN

2. ____   ATLANTA     4. ____   CANADA      6. ____   BRICKLAYER

**D. Concrete and Abstract Nouns:**
   **Directions:** Place a ☒ if the noun is abstract.

1. ____ fear 2. ____ faith 3. ____ fig 4. ____ forest

**E. Singular and Plural Nouns:**
   **Directions:** Write the correct spelling of each plural noun.

1. berry - _____ 5. replay - _____

2. tax - _____ 6. sofa - _____

3. mouse - _____ 7. gas - _____

4. deer - _____ 8. patch - _____

**F. Possessive Nouns:**
   **Directions:** Write the possessive.

1. room belonging to his sister - _____

2. an office used by more than one woman - _____

3. wading pool shared by two toddlers - _____

**G. Identifying Nouns:**
   **Directions:** Circle any nouns.

1. Three movies about birds of the desert were shown at our library yesterday.

**H. Punctuation:**
   **Directions:** Insert needed punctuation.

1. No we wont be moving to Purdy Washington

2. Kama asked  Was Emma born on Thursday May 20 1982

3. They hope to sell forty two tickets for our teams carnival by 4 30 today

4. By the way wash your ears face and neck with this suds free soap

5. His new address is 22 Brook Avenue Nyles MI  49102

**I.  Subjects and Verbs:**
    **Directions:**  Underline the subject once and the verb or verb phrase twice.
        **Note:**  Crossing out prepositional phrases will help you.

1.  A package from Emily arrived before dinner on Friday.

2.  A nurse and an aide helped the patient into bed.

3.  Four of the girls looked at the stars during the outdoor party.

4.  Come inside the house through the front door.


**J.  Contractions:**
    **Directions:**  Write the contraction.

1.  were not - _____
3.  I have - _____
5.  would not - _____

2.  they will - _____
4.  will not - _____
6.  what is - _____


**K.  You're/Your, It's/Its, and They're/Their/There:**
    **Directions:**  Circle the correct word.

1.  Take ( there, their, they're ) picture.

2.  I think that ( you're, your ) upset.

3.  Let me know when ( it's, its ) time to leave.


**L.  Subject-Verb Agreement:**
    **Directions:**  Underline the subject once. Underline the verb that agrees twice.

1.  Your idea ( sound, sounds ) interesting.

2.  The woman with the huge green glasses ( take, takes ) orders.

3.  His brother and she ( hikes, hike ) everywhere.


**M.  Irregular Verbs:**
    **Directions:**  Underline the subject once and the correct verb phrase twice.

1.  The dog was ( lying, laying ) on the porch.

2. Parker had ( rode, ridden ) her horse fast.

3. She has ( ate, eaten ) lunch.

4. I could have ( run, ran ) more than fifty yards.

5. We were ( given, gave ) large red markers.

6. My pencil is ( broke, broken ).

7. Have you ( did, done ) your homework?

8. We should have ( set, sat ) our lunches in the ice chest.

9. The bell may have already ( rang, rung ).

10. Kama's balloon had ( busted, burst ).

**N. Tenses:**
    **Directions:** Underline the subject once and the verb or verb phrase twice. Write the tense in the blank.

1. _____ The child colored a picture.

2. _____ You will turn left at the next street.

3. _____ Their dad is a beekeeper.

**O. Usage and Knowledge:**

1. Circle any infinitive that is a regular verb:   to flash    to fly    to flip

2. Circle the interjection:  **Wow!  This soup is hot and spicy.**

3. Circle the possessive pronoun:  **The girls are enjoying their new puppy.**

4. Write the antecedent of the possessive pronoun in sentence 3:  _____

5. Circle the conjunction:    **Yikes!  Mo or Bo has fallen in the stream.**

6. Circle the correct answer:  We haven't received ( no, any ) money.

7. Circle the correct answer:  My brother acts ( strange, strangely ) sometimes.

46

8. Circle the correct answer:   I didn't play very ( good, well ) in the first game.

9. Circle the correct answer:   Are you feeling ( good, well )?

**P.  Identifying Adjectives:**
    **Directions:**   Circle any adjective.

1. One elderly lady wore silver sandals with many stones and a low heel.

**Q.  Degrees of Adjectives:**
    **Directions:**   Circle the correct answer.

1.  The fifth storm was ( more violent, most violent ).

2.  This is the ( uglier, ugliest ) mask of the two.

3.  You are ( more creative, most creative ) than I.

**R.  Adverbs:**
    **Directions:**   Circle any adverbs.

1.  My friend talks too loudly sometimes.

2.  They never go anywhere early.

**S.  Degrees of Adverbs:**
    **Directions:**   Circle the correct answer.

1. Paco runs ( faster, fastest ) in his high school.

2.  Kit answers the phone ( more politely , mostly politely ) than his brother.

3.  When we travel, Aunt Jo stops ( more often, most often ) than Uncle Bo.

**T.  Pronouns:**
    **Directions:**   Circle the correct answer.

1.  ( Me and Lana, Lana and I, Lana and me ) made a clay pot.

2.  Don't hit Jacob and ( I, me )!

3.   The scouts must take ( his, their ) canteens.

4.   ( They, Them ) attend a rodeo every year.

5.   Our grandparents and ( we, us ) are going to Idaho.

6.   The baker fried the doughnuts ( hisself, himself ).

7.   Matt left with Sarah and ( she, her ).

**U.  Nouns Used as Subjects, Direct Objects, and Objects of the Preposition:**
      **Directions:**  Look at the boldfaced word.  Write **S.** for subject, **D.O.** for direct object, and **O.P.** for object of the preposition.

1. \_\_\_\_   During the **winter**, Tara skis.

2. \_\_\_\_   Give the **rattle** to the baby.

3. \_\_\_\_   After the parade, our **family** went to a café for lunch.

# Reflections

## Verb Test

_____

_____

_____

_____

_____

_____

_____

_____

_____

_____

_____

_____

# Reflections

## Preposition Test

_____

_____

_____

_____

_____

_____

_____

_____

_____

_____

_____

_____

# Reflections

## Noun Test

_____

_____

_____

_____

_____

_____

_____

_____

_____

_____

_____

# Reflections

## Adjective Test

_____

_____

_____

_____

_____

_____

_____

_____

_____

_____

_____

_____

# Reflections

## Adverb Test

_____

_____

_____

_____

_____

_____

_____

_____

_____

_____

_____

_____

# Reflections

## Pronoun Test

_____

_____

_____

_____

_____

_____

_____

_____

_____

_____

_____

_____

# Reflections

## Capitalization Test

_____

_____

_____

_____

_____

_____

_____

_____

_____

_____

_____

_____

# Reflections

## Punctuation Test

_____

_____

_____

_____

_____

_____

_____

_____

_____

_____

_____